The Island

Reminiscences of twentieth century
ranching on Santa Rosa Island

Pete Healey

ॐ

This book could not have happened without the inspiration of Al Vail, Bill Wallace, E.K. Smith and Jesus Bracamontes. Thanks to my brother-in-law Ed Smith and my wife Karen for the use of family pictures and to Marla Daily, Bill Dewey, Karen Foster Wells, Lulis Cuevas, and the Wallace family for their contributions. Thanks to Karen and Charlie for helping me sort pictures. Big time thank you to Bill Reynolds for his advice and putting this together. Most of all, thanks to The Island.

Cover photo caption:

Calves being unloaded off the Vaquero II early 1980s. These English cross cattle are from one of the northern states and were probably just taken off the cows and loaded in a snow storm then hauled for 24 hours to get to Port Hueneme, CA and then loaded aboard the boat and shipped 5 hours to The Island.

To the boys: Charlie, Eddie and Garrett

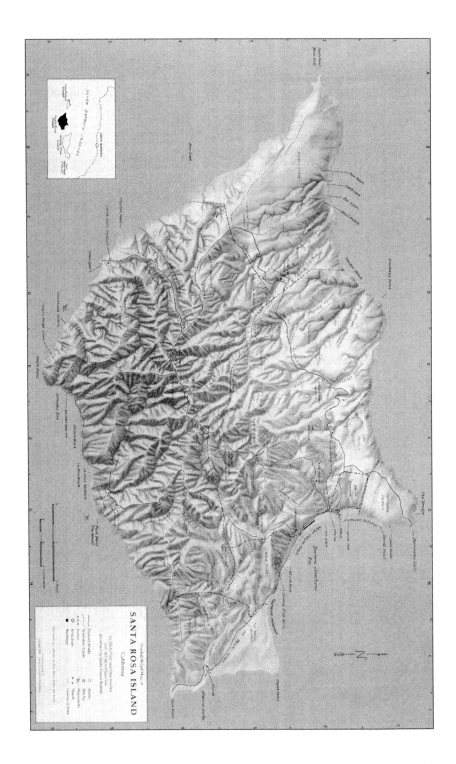

iv

Table of Contents

Foreword

In 1957 a popular West Coast, singing group named The Four Preps had a hit record with a song about an island off the Southern California coast. "26 Miles" was a catchy, sing-along tune about the romance that could be found on Santa Catalina Island – just "26 miles across the sea."

Ironically, another in the California Channel Islands chain, Santa Rosa Island was just 26 and *a half miles* "across the sea" and a bit further north. Its inhabitants, who ranched on The Island, lived a true storybook way of a life that, sadly, would soon disappear. "The Island" as it was simply called was home to a ranching partnership of members of two Arizona ranching families – the Vails and Vickers. The partnership started at the beginning of the last century and would end with the sale of their beloved Santa Rosa -the second largest of the Channel Islands – to the National Park Service in 1987. The cattle operation ended in 1988, followed by the ending of sport hunting in 2011. The sale was not without controversy or legal fireworks with transaction ending an era of the Channel Islands ranching saga.

Pete Healey's time with The Island started with family visits and vacations in the early 1970s and the stories you will read in this thoughtful little volume will lift you away to a simpler time and place where days were spent working horses and cattle and being centered around the idea that the ways of The Island and Mother Nature would always win. Pete's visual way of telling stories will entertain you and make you laugh, and maybe make you cry a little with the realization that a true pioneering way of life is gone. But have heart, these wonderful stories live and with them, the wisdom they impart.

At one time or another, we all dream of finding a place we can fly away to and live in the sun and wind in freedom and peace. Pete Healey was lucky to find his on "The Island."

—Bill Reynolds
Santa Ynez
2016

Introduction

The air on Santa Rosa Island has a unique intoxicating aroma, an earthy richness of salt air, grass and brush. When the wind is blowing fifty miles an hour you can get a lot of it, but there's nothing purer and you know exactly where you are. I was first imprinted with this smell at the age of twelve when my two brothers and I spent two weeks at the "Island" during summer vacation with my uncle who was the ranch foreman. It was a trip that would change my life forever. It would be there that I would learn my most marketable skills and where I would meet my wife. They say it takes a village to raise a child and The Island was my village, but this book is not about me.

Some of the events in this book are from my personal experiences and some are from stories that have been told to me. Although these stories concentrate on a few individuals, there could be countless stories written about the people of The Island like C.W. Smith, Ed Vail, Hayden Hunt, Diego Cuevas, Russ Vail, Margret Woolley, Sergio Marquez, and other cowboys that worked there from my generation and before, hopefully someday there will be.

The Island was once a vibrant and productive land. It supported thousands of cattle, a commercial herd of elk, deer, and wild pigs. It's rich biodiversity nourished countless species of insects, birds, and mammals including The Island Fox that thrived there. It's healthy mix of native and European grasses produced tax revenue through wages, cattle sold, hunting activities, and all of the mainland businesses that were needed to support an island ranch.

This was soon ended after its inclusion into the Channel Islands National Park. Was it for the greater good of The Island? According to the opinions of some, the answer is yes. In my opinion, today The Island feels as if it were a vacant lot. It has a history but it lacks life and the care that life requires. It's once rich grasslands are dead and heavy with carbon that cannot be sequestered into the soil.

It is unfortunate as The Island could have been both a national park and a productive ranching enterprise. It could have been a model for the rest of the world on how a unique, sensitive environment could be productive and protected at the same time. Like so many, The Island is deep inside of me. I miss The Island like the great men that I have written about in this volume but we have their stories.

—Pete Healey

The Island

Santa Rosa Island lies about 30 miles southwest of Santa Barbara, California and is the second largest of the eight Channel Islands. The Chumash people called The Island 'Wi'ma', which means redwood and their occupation lasted 13,000 years until the early 1800s. When first contacted by Juan Cabrillo in 1542, the native Chumash numbered in the hundreds, living in at least 9 coastal villages. Subsequent European contact in later centuries brought diseases which killed them off by the hundreds, as well as a major earthquake in 1812 that scared the rest into the mainland Spanish missions.

Ranching began about 1843 when The Island was ceded as a land grant from the governor of Mexico to Jose and Carlos Carrillo who in turn sold The Island to Carlos's daughters Manuela and Francisca. Both girls were married to Americans, John Jones and Alpheus Thompson who as business partners started the first ranching operation. In 1854 The Island was stocked with 270 head of cattle, 9 horses, 2 rams and 51 ewes. In 1858 the More brothers began acquiring interests in The Island and by 1881 A.P. More was the sole owner of Santa Rosa Island.

It was during the More era that the ranch took on its current appearance. They built several barns and two 2-story ranch houses, one which we called the 'Big House' is still standing today and is believed to be the oldest wood structure in Santa Barbara County. The two remaining barns are still in excellent condition, a testament to the workmanship of the era. Native flagstone was a common material used for foundations and may have been harvested from the ocean bluff when they were building the ramp down to the pier. More engineered a water system from Water Canyon for flood irrigation and planted a windbreak of Gum trees, which are all bent and curled to the east from the prevailing northwest winds. More ran primarily a sheep operation which numbered at one time about 100,000. The old sheep trails are still embedded in the hillside around the main ranch.

A.P. More died in 1893, having no children his estate was divided up between his siblings and their children. In 1901 Walter Vail and J.V. Vickers began buying interests in The Island under the name Vail and Vickers. Both Vail and Vickers began their cattle business' in Arizona. Walter Vail's start was from a pretty humble beginning when in 1876 he and two other partners purchased 160 acres with an old adobe house known as the Empire Ranch. The sale price was under $2,000.00 dollars and Walter had to borrow his third of the money from his uncle. Before the end of the century Walter would buy out his partners and acquire several thousand deeded acres as well as leased land. Some of this was with Vickers and was called the 'Panhandle Pasture Company'. By the turn of the century both men had expanded their enterprises into Southern California.

In 1902 Vail and Vickers began their cattle operation on The Island changing from the previous sheep enterprise of More. There was a considerable number of feral sheep

Aerial photo of the main ranch complex; The two barns on the left were built during the More era. Bunkhouse is upper right and the foreman's house is lower right.

left on The Island, at one point after 1914 when C.W. Smith became foreman he organized a gather and was able to corral a large number of sheep at the main ranch. The last of the feral sheep were killed off in the 1950s. Although Vail and Vickers had equal interests, the Vickers were silent partners with Vail doing the management until the partnership dissolved in 2011. Under Vail management The Island has been run primarily as a stocker operation although at times they ran a small cow herd on the west end of The Island which they stopped prior to 1960. A "stocker" is a weaned calf usually about 4-5 hundred pounds that is pastured on grass and grown to about 800 pounds plus, then they are either fed or sold as "feeders" to a feedlot where they are finished (fattened) to slaughter weight at about 1300 pounds. The feedlot thing didn't really happen until after WWII when there was a surplus of cheap grain and the American consumer was looking for a consistent beef product. At that time cattle were smaller and probably finished at 1000 plus pounds. Before WWII cattle were usually just grass finished and slaughtered right off pasture. Island cattle were brought in as yearlings and pastured until 3 or 4 years of age and then shipped into Wilmington where they were unloaded off the boat and walked right up to the slaughterhouse.

Typical to California, The Island was comprised mainly of winter annual grasses that were high in protein and then matured in the spring producing a carbohydrate rich grass. With only an average rainfall of 15 inches a year The Island can produce excellent grass and is a perfect fit for a stocker operation where cattle numbers can be increased during the growing "green" season and then destocked during the dormant season. Prior to 1980 most of the cattle were English type cattle mostly Hereford or Hereford-Angus cross bought from the northern states. At times southern cattle came in, these were cattle with Brahma-English cross or called "Crossbreds". In the most recent times most of the cattle anywhere are "Continental Cross", these are a mixture of European breeds that have a large frame. This is a product of 'production agriculture' that wants a big animal that can eat a lot of grain and get big.

On The Island operation, young weanling cattle were bought in the fall and winter and heavy two-year-old cattle were sold in the spring/summer. The bought calves would spend two green seasons on The Island or what is termed "doubled seasoned", and then sold as heavy feeders averaging about 1000 pounds. This worked well because of the logistics of an island operation which used a boat for hauling to town. The last boat the company owned was called the "Vaquero II" and could haul two truck-loads of cattle about 100,000 pounds. Cattle were shipped to Port Hueneme, CA. and then loaded into trucks for a feedlot destination usually out of state. The trip to town took five hours and the boat could make only one trip a day. It would take two months to gather and ship cattle in the spring with a crew of about eight cowboys and a remuda (saddle horses) of about sixty head.

Elk and deer were introduced sometime in the 20s. In 1978 a commercial hunting program began under the management of Multiple Use managers, this continued until 2011. In 1980 The Island was legislated into the Channel Island National Park and purchased in 1986. As part of the settlement Vail and Vickers would be allowed to continue operation until 2011. Because of unexpected restrictions by the National Park Service, the cattle operation lost the ability to be profitable and was terminated in 1998.

Two-year-old fat steers on board the Vaquero II headed to Port Hueneme.

Al Vail

Al Vail was the grandson of Walter Vail who had amassed a ranching empire in Arizona and California starting in 1876 until his death in 1906. Walter along with J.V. Vickers purchased Santa Rosa Island in 1901, forming the partnership of Vail and Vickers; Walter being the managing partner. Walter was killed in a street car accident in 1906 at the age of 54 and the management of The Island was passed down to his eldest son Russell who was Al's father. Russell managed The Island until his death in 1943 at which time his brother Ed took over until his death in 1962 and then Al was manager until his death in 2000.

The Vails had a reputation for being great cattlemen and Al was no exception, learning most of his trade from his Uncle Ed Vail and Island foreman C.W. Smith as well as others from the mainland ranches. I don't know how many thousands of head of cattle Al had sorted in his lifetime but he was a master at it. If a buyer bought a load of 1000 pound steers, that is what he got. Cattle that were cut to ship were weighed and it would not be uncommon to only see a 50-pound difference between each draft (a "Draft" is the number of cattle that would fit on the scale, usually 10-12 head of big cattle). Al used to say "I like to sell them the way I buy them", it was the old-school way.

The first time I met Al, although I really shouldn't say met, it was my first trip to The Island and I was twelve years old. There was a bunch of us kids and we had just come in off the boat and we were at my uncle's house wrestling on the floor when Al walked in. Al had a distinctive stiff legged walk like a man that was going somewhere. He was wearing his trademark blue denim shirt, white Levis, rough-out boots, and a short brimmed straw hat. As he stumbled over us kids on the way to the phone he growled "There's fifty-five thousand acres outside, go out there and play!".

Al was a great guy and probably the most honest person I have met in my life. He lived his life with complete integrity and there was no grey area, yes meant yes and no meant No! and a hand shake was a deal. Al admired hard workers with good common sense but distained ignorant, arrogant, and pretentious people. Researchers were often on The Island studying the flora and the fauna, these were smart people with big degrees but they sometimes failed Vail criteria. Al would say "These scientists are all alike, they're always late and when they pee it's into the wind".

Being manager, Al was at the mainland office most of the time except during the spring and fall round-ups when he was horseback with the crew. Al was a good cowboy and certainly not afraid of rough country. The Island was gathered in a systematic rotation designed by how the country was made up; Al and my uncle Bill who was the foreman would ride the outside circles ("circle" is an old term for gathering in cattle).

Al had a great sense of humor but really dry. In 1979 my cousin Rob was cowboying on The Island and he had a dog named 'Kid'. During the spring round-up we were riding through the Arlington Trap on our way to gather the Pocket Field and Al and Uncle Bill were in the lead with

Al Vail at the horse corral main ranch late 1930s or early 1940s.

the rest of the crew behind including Rob's dog. As we were trotting along, a fox jumped up out of the grass and ran in front of us. Kid saw the fox and started chasing it with Rob in hot pursuit trying to call him back but to no avail, the dog killed the fox. Rob was mad, he got down off his horse and with the dog in one hand and the fox in the other he started beating his dog with the dead fox. Meanwhile the rest of us were still trotting along behind Al and Bill. As we got up to the beating, Al looked over at Rob and without breaking stride he said "Rob, what are you going to do if that son of a bitch catches an elk?"

One time a guy came out to work but he wasn't very handy and he eventually quit. Al said to me "That guy did me a favor quitting; when he came to work it was just like two good men leaving".

Al used to give us younger guys what he called "Brownie Buttons" if we did something good, and he would take away brownie buttons if we screwed something up. If he needed one us to 'volunteer' to do something above and beyond the call of duty, he would give us a non-revocable brownie button. He loved it when somebody screwed something up so he could joke about it for days.

One year after the Fall round-up the whole crew left The Island to go to town for a few days except for me, I was the only one on the whole island. Talk about being by yourself! God knows I could find trouble to get into. Al was probably thinking the same thing so he flew out to baby-sit me for a couple of days. Both of us had nothing pressing to do. I had some chores around the ranch and I was working on building a saddle in my Uncle's shop. Al was catching up on his reading and watching golf. We did ride over to the Twin Peaks to walk some cattle home that had gotten missed during the gather which took some time. I did the cooking and no matter what I made Al thought it was good and ate it; the perfect roommate. When he left he said that if I would run everybody off he would come out every weekend.

I've been around a lot of cattlemen but none like Al Vail, he was the real deal. Al helped me out a ton of times for which I will never be able to repay him for, he taught me a bunch.

Al Vail sorting cattle Lepe Corrals 1979.

Bill Wallace

Bill Wallace is my mother's brother. My grandfather was a cowboy, horseshoer and horse trader and he kept all the kids busy riding young horses to sell which made them all pretty handy around rough horses. Bill first went to work on The Island in 1948 at the age of 20. He worked there five years until 1953. He returned in 1968 as the foreman and except for a two-year period from 1979 to 1981, was there until after the cattle operation shut down in 1998. Uncle Bill loved The Island, in his later years with his wife Meredith, he would often stay almost a year at a time without going to town.

The Island cattle operation and Bill Wallace were a perfect fit. Bill was an excellent horseman, cattleman, cowboy, carpenter, longshoreman, electrician, stone mason, saddle maker, or whatever. One year heavy swells (waves) tore a big section out of the middle of the pier. Usually the swells would just lift the decking off and we would put them back but this time they tore a section of stringers out from one row of pilling to another, about a 30-foot gap. I asked my uncle how we were going to fix the pier because I knew we didn't have any heavy lumber that thick or that long for stringers. He said "No problem we'll just make them". Uncle Bill's motto was 'do with what you have and you will never be with out'. This has served me well over the years.

Uncle Bill was my idol when I was a kid and I worshiped the ground he walked on. Bill was more of a father to me than an uncle. He taught me how to ride, work cattle, shoe horses, and build saddles. Most of all he taught me to do my best especially if you don't like what your doing, this has served me well over the years as well. As the foreman, he probably wasn't always liked but he was respected; he never asked anyone to do something he couldn't do himself.

Most of the real gentle ranch horses that us kids rode were usually made by my uncle. Bill's horses liked him and they liked working for him. During round-ups the saddle remuda at the ranch would number 60 plus head of horses and each cowboy would have about 6 horses in his string. We would bring them in daily to cut horses for that day or the next day work. Often when the horses came in the corral, Bill's horses would go up to him to visit before settling with the rest of the remuda. The Island was a horseback outfit with no trailers and a cowboy could ride a lot of miles in one day. Given that, not one horse in the remuda had a white mark on his back from a saddle burn; that was bad horsemanship and God save the person that cinch-sored a horse. One time we were saddled up and were just leaving the corral. One of the cowboys had just purchased a bridle called a 'mechanical hackamore', which is a leveraging device used to ride a horse in. My uncle got one glimpse of that and said "Get that bear trap off that horse." Needless to say that contraption never got used on The Island. My uncle used to say "Always make your horse as comfortable as possible". An example of this was one winter day; my uncle was stuck at the ranch by himself and he wanted to check the water in the dam at the Wire Field

Cowboy crew circa 1950; Bill Wallace on far right. Hayden Hunt sitting third from left cowboyed on The Island in the 1920s and was foreman from 1950 to 1958. Diego Cuevas sitting on the ground at left was Island foreman from 1958 to 1968.

which was a couple of miles down the coast but it was too wet to drive there. There was a group of older retired horses hanging around the barn so my uncle caught one of them. Being the horse was barefoot, Uncle Bill nailed some shoes on him, rode him down to check the dam and when he returned home he pulled off the shoes and turned him loose. My uncle would not ride a barefoot horse fearing the horse might get sore footed.

Some of my fondest memories are when it was just my uncle and myself on The Island. A single day might involve hunting pigs, fixing fence, fishing and riding colts. When I was working on The Island full time the rest of the crew would be in town during Christmas and it would just be my uncle and his family and me on The Island. Our Christmas ritual would be halter breaking colts in the morning and planting hay in the afternoon. The colts were about ten months old and range raised, never having had a human hand on them. Uncle Bill would rope them horseback and I would put the halters on them on the ground, needles to say it could get a little western. One year we did eleven of them.

One year right about New Years my brother whose name is also Bill came out to help us for a couple of weeks. We had a bunch of calves in and the crew was back from Christmas. My Uncle Bill and brother Bill decided that for a New Years resolution they would quit smoking. Well that day we took a couple hundred calves out of the Lobo Pasture and walked them up to the top of Black Mountain where there was a holding corral. They spent the night and then were walked to the back side of The Island the next day, their destination being Tranquillon Canyon. When we got to the corral on Black Mountain the next morning at daybreak there was a stiff gale out of the southeast and as soon as we turned the cattle out it started raining pretty hard. Well it was socked-in so hard you couldn't see fifty feet in front of yourself and of course these calves weren't driving very well. I thought when we got to the drift fence which was a couple of miles up and separated the front and back side of The Island that Uncle Bill would dump these cattle into the Arlington Country but he kept us going all the way to Tranquillon about another three miles over the top of The Island. When we turned the cattle loose in the bottom of the canyon the rain had subsided a little but everyone was soaking wet and cold. My uncle was standing beside his horse shaking uncontrollably from the cold; he looked at my brother and said "Goddammit Bill we sure picked a bad time to quit smoking".

Bill Wallace holding cattle. Bill made most all of the saddles and chaps used by the cowboys, he was also an excellent braider of rawhide reins and bosals.

E.K. Smith

The Smiths have a long history on The Island, Charles (C.W.) Smith was foreman there from 1914 until the mid-1940s. His son Edward K. Smith (E.K.) was born there in 1918 and was associated with The Island his entire life of 92 years. Both of his children and their children have been going to The Island their entire lives. E.K.'s son Ed is a park service employee and has spent most of the last 25 years doing maintenance on The Island. E.K.'s daughter Karen worked for Vail and Vickers both in the office and as a part time cowboy during round-ups. The first time I met E.K. was about 1974, I married his daughter Karen in 1990 and our son Charlie is named after C.W.

A person could have written a book about E.K. Smith; born on The Island, he went to school there until high school, he was a bomber pilot in the south pacific in WWII, a motorcycle cop in Santa Barbara, and then a sheriff deputy. After retiring from the sheriff department in the late 70s he worked part time for The Island, shipping and receiving cattle and as a deckhand on the boat. During the Fall and sometimes in the Spring he managed the mainland logistics for the commercial hunting operation on The Island.

E.K. had a rich history of an island ranch almost a hundred years ago. As a kid in the 1920s there wasn't any electricity or refrigeration. When they butchered a beef they would eat the meat that would stay fresh and the rest would be made into jerky that was stored in big wicker baskets at the bunkhouse kitchen. E.K.'s mother Cuca would soften this by pounding and then rehydrate with water and other ingredients to make 'machaca'. There were no motorized vehicles, everything was done horseback or with a wagon. He said they often took a wagon over to Lobo Canyon to get firewood. If they had to go down a steep hill they would put a timber through the spokes of the rear wheels to lock them up so they could slide the wagon down off a hill so it wouldn't run up on top of the two mules.

The Channel Islands is in the migratory route for Grey and Blue whales and E.K. said that he remembers the whales being so numerous at the end of the pier that a person could walk on them. During this time whaling was still prevalent and a whaling ship "the mother ship" would anchor in the channel between Santa Rosa and Santa Cruz Islands and it would send out several smaller boats to harpoon whales. E.K. said one time as a field trip from school on the Island they went out to visit the mother ship. I read in a history book somewhere that after they had gone out C.W. Smith told somebody that the crew on the ship was "The hardest looking sons of bitches" that he had ever seen. They must have been pretty rough because C.W. had seen quite a bit in his lifetime. E.K. said that during prohibition it was not uncommon to see a Coast Guard boat chasing a boat of rum-runners through the channel, sometimes the Coast guard would be shooting at them. Rum-runners often used the islands for drop-off points when smuggling booze to the mainland. E.K. used to tell a story about this when he was a kid. He said Juan Ayon, a

Sitting on one of the oxen circa 1920; E.K. Smith on left, C.W. Smith in center and Charlie Smith (E.K.'s older brother) on right. E.K. said he remembered there being two oxen on The Island when he was little, they used these to farm with.

long time Island cowboy, was down at the east end of The Island by Skunk Point (Old Ranch Pasture) and he sees some guys up from the beach burying something. He waited until they were gone then went down to see what it was and uncovered a bunch of booze. E.K. said he was up at the corrals when Juan came riding in 'three sheets to the wind'. He said Juan went right to work hitching up the wagon. By now the other cowboys at the ranch got wind of this so back down to the Old Ranch they went to get the load of booze. When they got back to the ranch the whole crew was drunk. E.K. said he didn't know what happened but they were all in the corral and all of a sudden they got in a big fist fight. He and the other kids were just sitting up on the fence watching with amusement until C.W. came up to put a stop to it. A few days later the owners of the booze came up to the ranch asking questions but C.W. told them he didn't know anything and they weren't going to mess with old C.W. so it was let go.

Loading cattle on a pier onto a moving chute into a boat can have its mishaps. Although rare it would not be unusual when running cattle down the pier to have a steer fall down and slide under the railing of the pier off into the water. One time when loading some cross-bred steers on a low tide in the dark before dawn, two steers jumped completely over the slide-rails of the chute into the water. A thousand-pound steer hitting the water from a twenty foot drop really makes a big splash. E.K. said one time when he was a kid he was helping two other cowboys run cattle down the pier. After the last draft of cattle, the other

E.K. Smith decking on the Vaquero II 1982.

two cowboys got off of their horses to help lift the chute up and untie the boat while E.K. sat on his horse next to the other two horses on the edge of the pier. When the two cowboys came back to mount up there was one horse standing with it's rump next to the head of the horse that E.K. was riding. As the cowboy was getting on that horse he swung his leg over and when he did his foot accidentally hit E.K.'s horse in the head causing him to rear up and fall over backwards off the end of the pier with E.K. on him. E.K. said "Boy that water was cold".

Jesus Bracamontes

Jesus was born in Sonora, Mexico in 1926. He came to The Island in 1952 and worked about 10 months then left and came back in 1962 and worked until the ranch closed in 1998. Jesus used to tell stories about when he was a kid in Mexico. His dad was a cowboy and rode young horses most of the time. Jesus said his dad would put him up on the front of the saddle with him and off they would go, if the horse got bothered and started to buck, Jesus's dad would throw him off in a bush. Once he got his horse straighten out, he would come back and pick him up. Jesus said they were poor and sometimes they would rope the neighbors' cattle and cut their tails off to make oxtail soup. Whenever we butchered a beef Jesus would always take the tail for soup. He would use the hide off of the tail to recover his saddle horn, like most of the Mexican cowboys he liked a slick rawhide horn.

Jesus was a big man, over six feet tall with broad shoulders, he was as tough as they come. His Indian features and thick mustache could make him appear as a pretty serious character but he was always quick with a laugh or a hug for us kids if we needed one. A good all-around cowboy, Jesus made good bridle horses that could do any job. I worked a lot with Jesus during my years on The Island and I can't tell you how many times he helped me out riding a young horse or if I got in a tight place working cattle. Jesus knew how to work cattle in rough country and when to be extra careful but if things got a little wild and reckless he was all in. I heard that one time when he was over on the south side of The Island he roped an elephant seal that was on the beach. The elephant seal headed for the water with Jesus and his horse in tow. Once they got to the water Jesus had to turn him loose, the big one that got away.

When I was about 19 years old, Jesus, Sergio Marquez, and I were over in the Pocket Field, a heifer pasture on the west end. We were riding the pasture looking for steers that had got through the fence from other country. We were split up and were going to meet at the old round-up grounds. I got there first and I was waiting next to my horse; there was a low hill on the west side and I see this big bull elk running full bore over the hill and in hot pursuit was Jesus. His hat was gone and he had his rope down. Within another fifty yards Jesus was up to him, he took a couple of swings and roped him around the horns. After he stopped him the elk made a couple of wild runs on the rope and then just sulled up. By this time Sergio was there and the two of us got loops on his feet and pulled him down. After we got him secured on the ground, I took a picture with my camera, Jesus ear-marked him, and we let him go.

I started working full time on The Island in January 1979, I was seventeen. On February 1st, my Uncle had sent me and Poncho and Sergio over to China Camp to spend a couple of days over there riding the country and checking on the cattle. It was wet as we had had some rain. The first night there we were awaken at midnight, it was Jesus, he

Holding down an elk that Jesus roped in the Pocket Field 1980.
Jesus Bracamontes on left and Sergio Marquez on the right,
Spook the dog is center.

was outside horseback. He told us that my grandfather had died and my uncle had sent him over to bring me back to the main ranch so that we could fly out in the morning. My grandfather had been gathering cattle in Nevada when he suffered a major heart attack and died on his horse. What's interesting is that my grandfather was helping a rancher who had sold a load of calves to Al Vail and these were going to be shipped to The Island.

While Jesus had a cup of coffee I went up to the corral and saddled my horse then we left for home. It was cold and clear that night and the stars were so brilliant that when we were riding over the top of The Island it was like we were in outer-space. Jesus had ridden three hours to get to China Camp and now it was another three hours back to the ranch. Nothing like a little six-hour ride in the middle of the night!

Another time during the winter we were riding the China Camp country, it was the whole crew and we picked up several heifers that had gotten out of the Pocket. When we got to the corrals and house at China Camp it was getting late and just starting to rain. It was decided that Jesus and I would stay at China Camp that night with the heifers and take them down the coast to the Pocket the next day while the rest of the crew would ride home that night. There wasn't much at the camp to eat except for some Graham Crackers and some canned fruit. Jesus found a bunch of wild mushrooms that he sautéed up in some Crisco. I don't know what he did to them but they were better than any French chef could make. There was a slow and steady rain most of the night and it was still drizzling when we left about daylight the next morning. We got down to the fence line at Bee Canyon that separates the Pocket Field from the Leppy country and put the heifers through the wire gate on the flat. There is a pretty good flat there, most of it on the Pocket side and it was a notorious place for airplanes to land on. Even though Jesus and I never said a word to each other we could see that there were fresh tracks in the grass from an airplane and just up the fence line there was a tent next to the fence with a .22 caliber rifle leaning against the fence. We tied our horses along the fence and I followed Jesus up to the tent. He grabbed the .22 and handed it to me then he pulled out a .38 caliber pistol that he had on his hip. Without saying a word, Jesus opened the tent flap and shoved the pistol inside the tent. There were three guys inside the tent and they yelled "Don't shoot, don't shoot". One of them looked at me and asked if I spoke English, I told them I did and I asked them what they were doing there. They said a boat had dropped them off and they were camping. So I asked them about the airplane tracks and the rifle. Jesus was still standing there with his gun out not saying a word. They fessed-up that a plane had dropped them off so they could hunt. I told them that we could have them arrested if we wanted. They were cold, hungry and Jesus had scared them pretty good. That was good enough for us so we left them there and rode home.

Cowboy crew circa 1960s. From left Mariano Romero,
Diego Cuevas, Justino Cuevas, Miguel Romero, Jesus Bracamontes
and Poncho Castillo.

Al and E.K.

Al Vail once said in an interview that he didn't know when he had met E.K. Smith because he couldn't remember not knowing him. When Al was a kid the whole family would often ride out to The Island on the company boat 'Vaquero' from Wilmington, the port they shipped cattle to and where they moored the Vaquero. Al, his twin brother Russ, and their sister Margaret would spend the weekends playing with The Island kids, among them E.K., his brother Charlie and their sister Francis. The Vail children would also spend time there during the summer when school was out. Al, Russ and E.K. were close friends and working associates until the end.

One of E.K.'s favorite stories was about he and Al when they were kids, I think they were pretty young maybe about 10 to 12 years old. The Windmill Canyon was right next to the ranch and it usually had cattle in it because it was a natural area for them to drift into and it had a water trough. Up the canyon a way there is a pretty good flat that is secluded and the boys would wander up there horseback and practice their roping. E.K. said that they made some break-away loops by using a piece of wire tied to the rope but sometimes this would get stuck and they would have to dally-up hard to break the rope loose. C.W. Smith was up at the windmill one day and noticed that there were a couple of steers with their horns broke so he asked the boys if they had been roping on the cattle which was a big no no. Of course, the boys were afraid to fess-up to the old man so they said no.

Soon after that they were up at the flat where there were some cattle laying around. At this time The Island ran steers that were just grass finished and they were often three or four years old, so they were big steers. So the boys started playing around the cattle with their breakaway loops. Well one of them got a loop around the head of one of these big steers and the rope wouldn't break away. They couldn't just let the steer go because he would be dragging a rope and if the old man saw it, it would have been certain death. The only way to get the rope off was for the other boy to rope the heels and then they could lay the steer down and take the ropes off. For two little kids this was a lot of work but they finally got the steer laid down and E.K. got down on the ground to take the ropes off. E.K. said he was so relieved to get the ropes off the steer but it was short lived, when he looked up he could see his dad sitting on his horse across the canyon in the Lobo pasture. C.W. had watched the whole thing. As short of a distance as it was, it was a long ride home for those two. I don't know if Al got a spanking but I'm sure E.K. did.

Horseback at the big house circa 1920s. From left Al Vail, E.K. Smith, Charlie Smith, Russ Vail and Margret Vail-Wooley.

Al and Bill

Al Vail and Bill Wallace first met each other in 1949. My uncle was working at the Alisal Ranch in Solvang, CA and his friend Jim Smith was going to Santa Barbara to interview for a job on The Island, so Bill went along. They met Al for a couple of drinks and they both got hired. Jim stayed for five months and Bill for most of his adult life.

Al and Bill were great working associates and also great friends. There was a mutual respect between them and together they ran a tight ship. It always amazed me how two people could have so much to talk about. Often we would leave the ranch horseback to gather the back side, it would take two to three hours to get where we were going and these two would talk the whole way.

I didn't know the two of them together until they were middle aged and pretty serious but I guess when they were younger back in the 50s they were a little wild and reckless. Back then the spring round-up was worked in one month rather than two when I worked there and the gathers were held and sorted in the open without the luxury of holding corrals. A day could start at 3:30 in the morning to ride to get where they needed to gather cattle, work country, cut cattle, walk cattle to a holding field, then change horses to make up a load of fresh cattle out of another field to ship that night. Sometimes they wouldn't get done loading the barge until midnight. If they happen to have any whiskey it wouldn't have been uncommon for the two of them to have a couple of rounds of drinks and just stay up instead of getting a couple of hours of sleep.

Booze on The Island was actually a rare commodity because once it was gone there was nowhere to get it so most of the time The Island was dry. Uncle Bill said one time they were unloading calves on the beach at Water Canyon and Al came over on the boat with them. Al was in a skiff to help steer the calves to the beach and in the skiff with him were his two suitcases. One had his clothes and the other had his supply of booze. There was a pretty good swell and as Al was coming into the beach a swell caught him and turned his skiff over. Uncle Bill said he could see Al diving down and then coming up for air and then diving down again. Al found the suitcase that had the booze in it and brought it to shore and let the other one go.

Like most big ranches The Island had it's fair share of rough horses and being a cowboy meant you could ride and do a day's work on them making good horses out of them. Tough country and hard work takes tough horses. Having a horse blow-up and buck was a daily event and it could happen in the dark leaving the corral in the morning or coming back to the corral in the dark that night. Uncle Bill used to ride a horse named 'Hornet'. According to his name I guess he wasn't a kid's horse. Uncle Bill said he would have to throw his jacket over his head to blindfold him so he could get on him in the morning. One night he was riding this horse to load the barge and he was bringing a draft of cattle coming down the alleyway to the pier when Hornet broke in two. Uncle Bill's saddle got loose and as they came down the little incline Hornet bucked the saddle over his

In front of the old Bunkhouse 1952. From left Al Vail, Diego Cuevas and Bill Wallace. The old bunkhouse built by More burned to the ground in 1969 killing the cook Howard Anderson.

head with Bill in it and as they went off they wiped off the hackamore on his head. Hornet was plumb naked and in the dark got in the middle of the cattle and ran down the pier into the loading pen with the cattle, luckily, they kept him from going down the chute onto the barge.

One season, the night before round-up was to start, Al initiated a bet with the whole crew. The terms were the first man to get bucked off during round-up would have to buy a case of whiskey for the whole crew. Three-thirty the next morning the crew was saddled up and ready to leave, the wind was blowing fifty miles an hour and it was pitch dark. Al threw open the gate to the corral and immediately his horse exploded bucking him off right in the gate opening. The next time the boat came out there was a case of whiskey on it for the crew.

Both Bill and Al smoked quite a bit at one time and when Al was cutting cattle he could be somewhat of a chain-smoker, lighting one cigarette off of the one he was finishing. If Nita Vail (Al's daughter) was working with us she would constantly be telling him not to light it. Uncle Bill smoked factory cigarettes and then also rolled his own out of pipe tobacco, his hands were the size of catcher mitts but they could roll the prettiest little cigarettes. There's a story that back in the fifties when Uncle Bill and Al were on The Island they had run out of cigarettes. A supply boat had come in but it couldn't get up to the pier to unload because of big swells so it was moored out on one of the cans (a can is a big metal buoy attached to an anchor chain and an anchor that it is used to tie boats off to). Both Al and Bill were accomplished swimmers and not wanting to wait any longer they stripped down at the end of the pier and swam out to the boat so they could have a cigarette. Al quit smoking altogether about 1980 after a horse fell over on him and broke several ribs, he said it hurt him too much to cough so he quit cold turkey and never smoked again. My uncle would quit off and on but finally gave it up after he retired and left The Island when the ranch folded up.

Uncle Bill told me a story one time when he and Al were over on the west end of The Island somewhere near China Camp. Some cattle were down on a beach between two rocky points, being concerned about them getting stuck down there during high tide they slid down the trail the cattle had made onto the beach. The trail down to the beach wasn't very good to begin with and after they had climbed the cattle back up it to the flat these cattle had pretty much obliterated the trail making it so Al and Bill couldn't get their horses back up it. Their only choice was to swim their horses around one of the points and come up on the next beach over which had a trail out. Uncle Bill said his horse was a good swimmer but Al's horse wouldn't swim, he would go down under the water bounce off the bottom then come back up and get some air and then go down again. Being as Al was fully clothed with boots, chaps, and spurs on he had no choice but to hang onto the saddle and go with him and do the same thing. Needless to say they made it around and probably headed over to the shack at China Camp where they could dry off a bit.

Another time when water was an obstacle was one winter. The crew had moved a bunch of calves from the Wire Field over into the San Augustine Canyon and it began to rain heavily. By the time they had settled the cattle and rode back over the south road the rain had flooded Water Canyon making it unable to pass horseback. Since they were soaking wet and the crossing at Water Canyon was close to the beach they decided to just jump off into the flooded canyon and let the water take them to the ocean where they could go ashore on the ranch side of the beach and then take the road from the barge landing up to the airstrip and then home. Everyone jumped in except Juan Ayon who chose to ride back to the top of The Island between Las Cruces and the Wreck then ride over Quinn's Knob to the top of Water Canyon and back over Black Mountain to the ranch, probably another 3 to 4-hour ride.

Weighing cattle at the scale house late 1990s. Al Vail and Bill Wallace.

Bill and Jesus

Bill Wallace and Jesus Bracamontes first meet each other in 1952 when Jesus came out to work a few months which included the spring round-up and shipping. That year they loaded the last load of cattle on the barge which is what they called a clean-up load. This was made up of a variety of cattle that didn't fit the other cattle going into the feedlot because of their size or they had something like a lump jaw or a bad leg. Instead of being sold into load lots these would go to the sales yard to be sold individually.

As the boat was towing the barge heading toward the back side of Santa Cruz Island it broke loose and went ashore on the west side of Santa Cruz just south of Christi Ranch. They got the cattle unloaded to a beach and then they pulled the barge off. Damage from hitting The Island had caused a pretty good leak and it was taking on quite a bit of water. Uncle Bill said he and Al pumped and bailed water all the way around the backside of Santa Cruz but it finally sank on them when they got abreast of Anacapa Island where they cut it loose.

Bill and Jesus were sent over to Santa Cruz to keep track of the cattle until transportation could be arranged to get them off The Island. Uncle Bill said he didn't speak much Spanish and Jesus didn't speak much English. The main ranch gave them a couple of horses to use. Uncle Bill said they were a couple of broken down old nags. Christi Ranch has a couple of old adobe houses built way back and Bill and Jesus used one of them as a camp where they cooked over the fireplace. Uncle Bill told me they had enough provisions for a week, they were there for a month with no word from anyone. Desperate for food they would hunt the feral sheep that roamed the west end of The Island. Uncle Bill had an old .45 caliber pistol with him but the hammer on the gun was slightly bent and wouldn't always fire the bullet. One day they got a young lamb hemmed-up in a draw and Uncle Bill was going to shoot it with his pistol but the gun wouldn't fire, Jesus came to the rescue and hit the lamb over the head with a rock to kill it. Thirty years later they both said it was the best lamb they had ever eaten. Things always taste better when your starving.

Laying in their bedrolls they were awakened in the middle of the night by Al Vail. He had ridden over to Christi and all he had with him was a bottle of whiskey. The three of them drank the bottle of whiskey and the next morning at daylight they gathered up the cattle and drove them over the mountain into the valley and down to Prisoners Harbor to get shipped to town.

Cowboy crew circa 1974.
From left: Mariano Romero, Chuey Jimenez, Bill Wallace,
Jesus Bracamontes, Chilo, Bobby Romero, unknown. The red barns
were built during the More era in the late 1800s. The metal tank was
used during this time to render tallow off of sheep carcasses.

Spook

My Uncle always had a dog or two. When I first went to The Island there were two dogs; Minnie and Poncho. Minnie was a little female terrier and Poncho was a big mixed breed dog of unknown descent. The two of them had wandered off one time and Al found them over in the Pocket Field which is on the other end of The Island. Al said they must have been hungry because when he ran across them they were eating grasshoppers. Minnie was the toughest little dog that God had ever created, she had been known to kill some pretty good size pigs by grabbing them by the throat. One thing she liked to do was jump out of the back of the pick-up truck when we were a long way from the ranch and run home. She knew all the short cuts. It would not be uncommon for us to get home after driving an hour and here would come Minnie fifteen minutes later running in.

Minnie stayed at my uncle's house but if Al came to The Island she would switch camps and go stay with Al. Al liked 'Butterfinger' candy bars and he would share them with Minnie so she would bunk with Al. This used to amuse Kenny Oppel the boat skipper. Kenny would chastise her and say "Minnie, you little Slut".

One of Al's cattle buyers gave my uncle an Australian Shepard pup. At first this pup was extremely timid and scared so my uncle called him 'Spook'. Spook had a great personality and he was smart although he could do some stupid things. When he was young he would go on every gather during round-up. One season we were working the Lepe country on the back side of The Island. This was the second to the last gather and Spook had made quite a few miles up "til then and he was tired. Uncle Bill and I were trailing a bunch of cattle up a narrow canyon to the corrals and Spook was right behind the last steer dogging along with his tongue out and his head right between the steer's hind legs. The steer lifted his tail and pooped a slushy green cow pie right on top of Spook's head. All poor Spook could do was stop and wipe the green slim out of his eyes and then continue on.

As Spook got older he would watch which direction we were leaving the barn on horseback to decide if he wanted to go or not, he didn't want to make a mistake and go on a long circle (gather) but sometimes he would screw-up and end up on one. When he got to being an old dog he would go to the barn to saddle up with Uncle Bill and then he would go home. When we brought cattle in to make up loads for the boat he would come over from the house and bite a few steers up the ally and then go home. One job he always did though was help load the boat. He had his own spot where the lead-up chute joined the chute that went onto the boat. Spook never barked and he would only bite cattle if they got stalled out or jammed up. He actually worked his spot better that a person could. Al once said that if that dog could talk he would run these "cowpunchers" off. Another place he liked to work was over at the squeeze chute where we processed cattle for branding and vaccinations. Again he was very meticulous about keeping the flow of cattle efficient.

When my Uncle and his family made a trip to town I would stay up at their house so I could babysit Spook. He would usually sit around and sulk for a couple of days after they left before he would start hanging out with me. At night I would leave the front door cracked for him in case he had to go out to do any business. One night I was asleep and he came in the bedroom and stuck his nose under the blankets to wake me up, he wanted something. When I was getting ready to ask him I noticed that there was no light coming from the hallway and there was always a shimmer of light from a lamp that was on my uncle's bar that he keep on 24-7. So I got up to check the lights and everything was off and I could see out the window that the barn lights were off as well. This meant that the generator had shut off and that's what Spook was trying to tell me. So I got dressed and I went up to the shop and sure enough the generator had shut off so I fired-up the other generator (we had two) and I went back to the house and back to bed.

I was awakened out of sleep again by Spook's wet nose under the blanket poking me. At first I thought the generator was off again but I could see light in the hallway from the bar light in the living room so I ignored Spook and tried to go back to sleep. There was that wet nose again, this time it had a little urgency to it so I got up. This made Spook happy and he led the way out the bedroom door into the hall and then he immediately stopped at the end of the bar. Well when he stopped I did too and not a foot from me standing on the bar looking me in the eyes was a big Island skunk. There was nothing I could really do about that so both of us retreated to the bedroom, the skunk was gone in the morning.

Spook liked riding in the pick-up, he would even ride on a boat but he loved helicopters. I don't know what got him started on it but if a helicopter landed at the ranch Spook wanted to go for a ride. Charlie McLaughlin from Aspen Aviation would fly in quite often with Park personnel, sometimes he would have a senator or a congressman with him. Whenever he landed on the flat by my uncle's house, Spook would run over to the helicopter and Charlie would throw him in and take him for a ride.

When Spook died, Uncle Bill buried him over by the squeeze chute, one of Spook's favorite places.

Spook fixing fence circa 1980s. Jesus Bracamontes and Sergio Marquez. The elk were hard on fences and it would be common for a large bunch of them to destroy 50 yards of fence line.

Time and Taking Time

There is standard time, daylight saving time and then there is Vail time. Vail time means be there at least 15 minutes early. Al Vail was a stickler for being on time, no doubt training from his youth.

E.K. Smith used to tell the story about when his dad C.W. was foreman. Back then The Island had a supply boat called the 'Onward' which stayed at The Island. Once a month C.W. would bring the crew in for a weekend in town and to get supplies. C.W. would tell the crew that they would be leaving at 3:00 on the Monday morning. Well 3:00 meant 3:00. E.K. said "The old man would have the boat ready to go and there would be headlights coming down the pier, a taxi bringing one of the cowboys down to get on the boat. The old man would be looking at his watch and when it said 3:00 he would tell us to turn the boat loose". The late cowboy would be left in town for another month without pay.

Santa Cruz Island is one of the neighboring islands to Santa Rosa and prior to 1988 was a cow-calf ranch. As a common practice Al would buy some of their calves for The Island's stocker operation. Being close by we could haul two loads of cattle on our boat the 'Vaquero II' which was designed to hold two truck-loads of cattle or 100,000 pounds. If the boat was short a deckhand, it was not uncommon for one of the cowboys to work as a deckhand and I worked on the boat quite a few times.

The pier on Santa Cruz Island sits in a bay called Prisoners Harbor. Except for when a northeast wind was blowing this is a nice harbor like being at a lake jetty. The pier is pretty short and it only took two lines to tie the boat up whereas on Santa Rosa the pier is probably at least three times longer and almost always there was wind and a swell. On Santa Rosa we used four lines to hold the boat in and the chute was on rails so it could move up and down and sideways. Because we wanted to keep the boat from banging against the pier as little as possible, unloading or loading cattle on Santa Rosa was fast and efficient like a well-oiled machine. In bad weather, the less time the boat was tied to the pier the better, this saved wear and tear on the boat and the pier.

One fall we were picking up cattle at Santa Cruz Island and Al was on the boat. Although he found it humorous, Al was always annoyed at the lack of efficacy at Santa Cruz; they were never prepared and it took them forever to get something done. This day was the same deal; they didn't have the bow line down at the pier to tie the boat up and when we finally got going the crew bringing the drafts down were not starting the cattle right and the calves were turning around on the pier not wanting to load. Al was standing up on the catwalk that ran lengthwise and above the pens on the boat, he yelled over to Carey Stanton, the owner and said "Hey Carey, can't you speed those boys up a little?". Carey, a meek, soft-spoken person said "Well Al, the pier is kind of wet and I don't want a horse to fall and break somebody's leg". Al immediately shouted back

"Goddamit, there's a lot of good doctors in town".

During round-ups we would often leave the ranch horseback at 3:30 or 4:00 in the morning so we could get to the country we needed to gather by daylight, only to sit on top of the mountain for several hours until the fog cleared. Once we started working cattle there was no time constraints, cattle were never rushed and whatever couldn't get done in the daylight that day was finished the next if need be. One time that comes to mind was when we were working the China Camp Round-up on the back side of The Island. This was always a long day anyway. We had gathered and sorted cattle and were walking the heavy steers from the coast to the Lepe corrals where they would overnight. Climbing out of Whetstone canyon a couple of steers started to get a little tired and hot so Al held the cattle up on the hillside, this was about 6:00 in the evening. We waited there about an hour until Al was satisfied that the cattle were good and then we went on to the corral which was about a half mile away.

When walking cattle anywhere it was always necessary to settle the cattle when you got to where you wanted to go and usually on water. Nothing like waiting to settle cattle with the fog and wind blowing fifty miles an hour. As my uncle would tell me, you never leave walking cattle or they will just keep walking, that just adds stress to the cattle. Some of these things you don't really appreciate until you own your own cattle.

Talking about fog. Al and Bill always laughed about the time they went up to gather the Carrington Point. This pasture is right next to the ranch headquarters. When they got up there the fog came in so they had to wait for it to clear so they could see to gather. They waited three hours sitting there before they could go to work. As they got older, Al and Bill would wait until we could see the fog clearing on Black Mountain before we left the ranch. On those foggy mornings, Al would say to Bill "Hey Bill, remember when we sat in the fog on the Point for three hours and we were only 15 minutes away from the coffee pot".

Taking cattle back to La Jolla after working them at the Wreck Corrals, fall inventory 1984.

Wild Pigs

Both Santa Cruz and Santa Rosa Islands have had wild pigs on them since nobody really knows when. Some think when the Europeans were exploring the islands that they left some pigs so when they were passing through they could stop and hunt fresh meat. Most reasonably they were pigs that had gone feral from the early ranching period during the Mexican land grants. The pigs on Santa Catalina Island came from Santa Rosa in the early 1930s. The islands traded pigs for quail. Although the Pigs are gone from Santa Rosa, the Catalina quail are still there. E.K. Smith remembered when they were catching the pigs for Catalina, they would rope some young ones and then tie their feet together and pack them back to the ranch horseback. The exact numbers I don't know.

Because wild pigs are so prolific they were always a management problem trying to keep their numbers controlled. Very rarely did we ever leave the ranch without packing a rifle to shoot pigs with. The only time we didn't carry guns was during round-up when we were gathering. Al and Bill didn't want us off getting occupied shooting pigs when we should be working cattle.

During the 1950s they introduced a swine cholera into the pigs to try and depopulate them. To do this they would rope a pig to catch it and then give it an injection with the cholera virus. Uncle Bill said they were down in the Wreck Canyon and they caught a big boar hog. The Wreck is a rough and rocky canyon from top to bottom, he didn't say exactly where they were but anyplace wouldn't have been good. Anyway they roped this boar down in the creek bottom where he got all tangled up down there. He said they messed around with that pig for about an hour before they finally got him stretched out and got an injection in him. Well they turned the pig loose and he ran up behind one of the horses and the horse kicked him in the head and killed him.

Juan Ayon was a long time island cowboy. What I've heard is that he came up from the Empire Ranch in Arizona with C.W. Smith in 1914 and worked on The Island until the late 50s. Uncle Bill said that when he had worked with Juan back in the early 50s that Juan had made a new reata. A reata is a long lariat or rope made out of braided rawhide. These take many hours to make; preparing the hide, cutting the strings, and braiding. The strings are cut in a circular fashion around the hide to produce a continuous string. The reata usually consists of four continuous strings braided together so there is no splice which creates a weak spot.

The first time Juan packed his new reata, he and Uncle Bill had gone down to the Old Ranch to look at some cattle. On the way home they jumped a big hog at Indian Canyon and Juan roped him with his new reata. I guess Juan had a little trouble handling his rope, he got too much slack in it and the pig ran back through the middle of the reata and bit it clean in two. The hog got away and took half the reata with him.

One winter when I was working on The Island there

Loading a tied-up pig to take back to the ranch circa 1930.
Pigs were traded to Catalina Island for quail. The cowboy
standing is probably C.W. Smith.

were a lot of pigs and they were tearing up the south side country pretty bad. Uncle Bill decided that we would work the San Augustine and Wreck horseback and shoot as many pigs as possible. There was about six of us and we divided the country as if we were gathering and worked it down and over to the Wreck corrals. Altogether we shot about two hundred pigs. It was early afternoon when we got to the Wreck corrals and we had a late lunch of coffee with graham crackers and peanut butter. Uncle Bill sent the rest of the crew home but he wanted to ride around the south side to Johnsons Lee to see the cattle and the country then come home over the top of The Island. This was a pretty long ride but I was riding a good stout horse so I told him I would go with him.

It was late afternoon and just starting to get dark when we jumped a big boar coming along the road at the top of Soledad Mountain. We both jumped down and got our rifles out. Uncle Bill was to the left of me and so was the hog so I let him shoot first. He made a good shot and the pig ran across the road to the right and into a swale. Uncle Bill put his rifle back into the scabbard, mounted up and rode over to make sure the pig was dead. Besides having a rifle my uncle was packing a brand new semi-automatic .22 caliber pistol that a friend of his had given him. He had been carrying this pistol in a holster on his hip all day and hadn't used it yet. I had remounted and I was sitting on my horse about fifty feet away, my uncle rode just uphill from the pig and he pulled out his pistol to finish him off. He fired one shot and then he stuck the pistol back into the holster but he was having trouble getting it back in. I could see him jerking the pistol up and down and then "Bang!" It went off. Uncle Bill had a confused look on his face, he nonchalantly pulled his hip over with his right hand to look at his butt and said "goddamit Pete, I shot myself in the ass".

Because of my lack of maturity and the fact that this was so unbelievable, I started laughing. I asked him if he was kidding me and he said "No" and he turned his horse down the road and we headed for home. Even though he never said a word, it must have hurt because he stood up in his stirrups most of the way home. This just added to my uncontrollable giggling and we had a good five to six miles of trotting to get back to the ranch. Coming down Black Mountain he did look at me and told me not to tell anybody, trying to control myself, I told him I wouldn't. When we got home I told Uncle Bill that I would take care of the horses while he went up to the house. After I had unsaddled and turned the horses out I went up to the house to help my uncle with his wound. The bullet had gone through the outer part of the cheek of his butt about six inches and came out. The bullet had struck the cantle of his saddle and stayed inside his pant leg and ended up in his boot. It was a nice clean wound so I got a syringe full of hydrogen peroxide and pumped it through the upper hole and flushed it out the bottom.

I kept my word and didn't say anything to anybody, but when uncle Bill came limping into the bunkhouse kitchen the next morning for coffee I started laughing. My uncle was a good sport and told everybody what happened. From then on he always referred to that pistol as his 'ass shooting gun'.

Dead boar in back of a jeep in front of the old bunkhouse circa 1950. From left: Diego Cuevas, Bill Wallace and Margo Turner. Diego has the brim of his felt hat cut into the shape of a ball cap for less wind resistance.

Wind

You can't really talk about Santa Rosa Island without mentioning the wind. When More built the ranch headquarters in the 1800s at Bechers Bay, he planted an L shaped row of Blue Gum trees as a wind break but also as the story goes to be used for pulling in the pier. These trees are anything but straight from the relentless northwest winds that can gust over 60 miles an hour during the spring and summer. I have been told that weather instruments have clocked the wind at 120 miles an hour on top of Soledad peak. I can personally remember two occasions when we were gathering cattle on top of The Island when the wind had lifted me out of the saddle.

Wind can raise hell with a western hat and that's why most of the crew used to wear ball caps or a narrow-brimmed hat. One of the cowboys named Arturo Teran even had a "Stampede String" on his ball cap to prevent the wind from sucking it off. Al used to laugh about one time when his uncle, Ed Vail and a couple of other guys had just arrived by boat at The Island and the wind was really blowing. One of the men stuck his head outside the wheelhouse and he immediately lost his hat into the ocean. The other guy couldn't believe the wind was that hard so he attemped to look outside and he also lost his hat into the ocean. Ed Vail scorned the two as "sissies' for not being able to keep their hats on but when he went outside he immediately lost his hat too. E.K Smith said that he and Ed Vail used to wear the same hat size and if

Ed happened to lose his hat he would take E.K.'s to wear and leave him hatless.

When we were shipping cattle off The Island, we would often ship for a few days in a row. The trip to Port Hueneme would take five hours one way and the boat would probably spend an hour tied-up at the Santa Rosa wharf while the cattle were unloaded and then loaded into trucks. Being stuck on the boat for a long period of time, the boat crew (the skipper and deckhand) would sometimes come in to have dinner at the bunkhouse. To do this they would leave the boat on its mooring which was about a hundred yards off the pier and row a skiff up to the pier which they would tie off there then walk up to the bunkhouse. If the wind was blowing too hard they usually wouldn't attempt it as it was almost impossible to row against the wind.

The Smith's (E.K., Angie, Karen and Ed) came out to The Island every summer right after the kids got out of school as long as E.K. wasn't needed in town to receive cattle at Port Hueneme. They were there one year and E.K. was down on the pier when we were loading and he invited Kenny Opple who was the boat operator at that time and Jim Preston who was the deckhand up to dinner with them at the Big House that night. When the boat got back to The Island that afternoon the wind was blowing pretty good but Kenny and Jim made it in fine in the skiff. They went up to the house to eat, I'm sure E.K. and Angie put on a good spread and of course they had to have a couple of martinis. After dinner, they probably had a night-cap and it was after dark when E.K. drove them down to the end of the pier to get on the skiff. Once they were aboard the skiff E.K. left and went home. Kenny had probably rowed out to the boat hundreds of times during the sixteen years he had run the Vaquero II but he and Jim had a little trouble that night. The wind was blowing at gale force and as they got to the boat it pushed them away from it so they were unable to grab on to anything. The next thing they knew they were behind it and no way could they row against the wind swell. Their only option now was to row like crazy to get to the beach or end up in San Diego somewhere.

They ended up getting to the beach at Water Canyon about 1.25 miles down the coast and as they were coming in a wave swamped the skiff getting them both wet. From there they walked back to the ranch. What time I don't know. All I know is when we were getting up at 3:30 the next morning Al was down at the bunkhouse and he had a funny smile on his face. Kenny was in the bathroom wringing his socks out in the wash basin, he was not in a good mood. Al took a couple of the boys down to Water Canyon to get the skiff and take it to the pier so Kenny and Jim could get to the boat. Of course, no mishaps this time. This delayed getting the boat loaded at the usual time but we weren't too late and Al wasn't upset about it because the whole incident gave him great amusement. Life on a ranch especially one in the ocean is about amusement over mishap.

A little note about Kenny Opple, he was a great guy and probably one of the best boat skippers there ever was. He drank warm Coors beer and there wasn't an ocean that was too rough for him.

The wind on The Island was a way of a life and although it could get tiresome at times it was somehow different than the wind on the mainland which can be annoying. The best nights of sleep I ever had was on The Island when the wind was rattling the windows of the house.

The cattle boat Vaquero II at Santa Rosa Island.
Built in 1959, it was sold after the cattle operation ended.

Epilog

As part of the inclusion into the Channel Island Nation Park in 1987 Vail and Vickers were granted a lease agreement until the year 2011 to continue the cattle and commercial hunting operations. Because of increasing restrictions placed upon the cattle operation this was terminated in 1998. All of the cattle were shipped off and most of the horse herd except for some retired horses and a group of gentle horses for the family. All of the cowboys were shipped in with the last of the horses except for Sergio Marquez and my uncle and their families.

Bill Wallace and his wife Meredith moved off the Island and up to Chico California in April 1999. He died in July 2015 at the age of 87. We talked often and he always wanted to know what was going on at the Island. He never went back and I know he mourned the Island every day of the sixteen years that he lived in town.

Even though the cattle were gone, Al Vail continued as active manager of the company. Al died January 4th 2000 from a heart attack while at the office, he was 78 years old. Karen called me with the news, it was one of those calls I won't forget.

E.K. Smith died in May 2010 at the age of 92. He was a goer to the end. He always enjoyed being on the Island more than anywhere especially when friends and family were there.

Jesus Bracamontes is reported to still be alive and living in Mexico, he would be 90 years old.

After the lease expired in 2011, friends and family no longer had the privilege to go to the Island unless as campers with the general public. There are still a few head of horses left that the park service has to provide care for and because of that I am hired once or twice a year to trim their feet. Karen and Charlie go with me on these trips and often we plan them when Karen's brother Ed is working on the Island and has his wife Suzan and their twin boys Eddie and Garrett with him. The boys love the Island and more than once we have had to pry them off the wind-swept beach after they had been playing for hours only to hear them say "What, we just got here".

I know that there are probably several members of the Vail family that could have the opportunity to revisit the Island but I don't think they would as the heartbreak would overweigh the visit back. I know the trips back are hard on my wife but aside from tending to the horses I need my fix. The aroma of the Island air is like oxygen to a dying man. There is nothing like being on a ridge top in pure quiet only broken by the sound of waves crashing and sealions barking on the coast a couple of miles away.

There is a place on the Island I used to go to three times a year when we were gathering cattle. Way down on the coast of the Sierra Pablo on the south side. It's a long way down off the main ridgeline and a long-haul walking cattle back out. We all had designated country that we worked and mine was a couple of ridges that ended up on a little flat at the ocean. There is an ancient Chumash Indian camp there, depressions in the ground that were once their house pits, shell midden littered in the sandy soil. Invariable I always jumped out a big buck lying in the brush, this country was a good place to become a big old buck. After checking for signs of cattle I would dismount to 'shake my saddle', loosening the cinches and lifting the back of my saddle up to air my horse's back. Standing there I would gaze at the endless ocean with the morning sun low in the sky and I would 'chill out'. There was something spiritual about this place, maybe that's why the Indians camped there. I have told my wife that I want my ashes scattered there when I die. I haven't been to that spot in years and will probably never see it again but I can go there in my mind.

We value our trips to the Island because we know someday they will end. Even though the ranch is in ruins, the Island is still "The Island" and the most beautiful and peaceful place on this earth that we know.

Al Vail and C.W. Smith probably early 1940s.

C.W. Smith center with Standard Oil crew 1932.

Al Vail

Walking cattle home out of Green Canyon.

Looking east toward Skunk Point, Santa Cruz Island is on the left.

Justino Cuevas and E.K. Smith at the meat house 1954.

Unloading calves 1985.

The Vaquero I (built 1913) unloading yearlings into the water circa 1930. The pier was in disrepair due to big waves that had torn off the A-frame and chute. The Vaquero was taken by the government in 1942 for service in the South Pacific during WWII.

Claude Morris, Al Vail and Ray Lopez, late 1930s.

*Karen Smith-Healey, Pete Healey, Nita Vail, Ed Smith, Tom Mullins,
E.K. Smith at Green Canyon Corrales, 2000.*

Herding cattle to shore in a skiff, circa 1930.

Brood mares at the Old Ranch, *painting by Karen Foster Wells.*

East Beach *painting by Karen Foster Wells.*

E.K. Smith unloading fat steers at Port Hueneme, 1990s.

E.K. Smith with the grand kids, Garrett Smith, Charlie Healey and Eddie Smith, East End 2006.

La Jolla Beach 2005. Front row from left Garrett Smith, Angie Smith, Charlie Healey, Eddie Smith. Back row from left Ed Smith, Suzan Smith, Pete Healey, Karen Healey, E.K. Smith.

E.K. Smith at the East End 2006.

Grave stone for Juan Ayon at the Calvary Cemetery in Santa Barbara CA. Juan came from the Vail's Empire Ranch in Arizona and worked on The Island for 42 years.

The Vaquero I loaded with heavy cattle, at 130 feet long this boat could hold four carloads (truck loads) of cattle. Standing on the deck are Nita Vail and N.R. Vail, Al's parents. Often during shipping season the Vails would board the boat on a Friday night after the kids got out of school and make the eleven-hour trip to The Island arriving at daybreak, spend the weekend and then ride the boat back to Wilmington arriving early Monday morning in time to go to school.

The Vaquero II coming alongside the pier to offload supplies circa 1960s.

Spring round-up crew of 1935 lined up in the barn corral. C.W. Smith 6th from left and Charlie Smith (E.K.'s older brother). Charlie died the following year from an accidental gun shot while at the Jalama Ranch near Point Conception, CA, he was 21 years old.

Pete Healey

Karen, Charlie and Pete Healey

Pete Healey's first trip to Santa Rosa Island was in 1973 at the age of 12. Summer vacations turned into employment when he joined the cowboy crew at the age of 17. Pete would work on and off The Island for the next nine years and continual seasonal employment until the last of the cattle were removed in 1998. In 1994 Pete started a horse-shoeing business in the Santa Barbara area along with some other business ventures. Pete married Karen Smith in 1990 and their son Charlie was born in 2002.

Pete is the manager of Healey Enterprises, LLC which includes the farrier business, a seasonal cattle operation and a company that sells measuring systems for horses' feet. Pete is the CEO of an emerging non-profit corporation called the Equine Podiatry Education Foundation that is involved in collecting research data for the equine foot. The Healey's live in Santa Ynez, California.

Made in the USA
San Bernardino, CA
17 April 2017